The Word was God

Published by
The Bible Reading Fellowship
15 The Chambers, Vineyard
Abingdon OX14 3FE
United Kingdom
Tel: +44 (0)1865 319700
Email: enquiries@brf.org.uk
Website: www.brf.org.uk
BRF is a Registered Charity

ISBN 978 0 85746 424 8
First published 2015
10 9 8 7 6 5 4 3 2 1 0

Acknowledgements
Unless otherwise stated, Scripture quotations taken from The Holy Bible, New International Version (Anglicised edition) copyright © 1979, 1984, 2011 by Biblica. Used by permission of Hodder & Stoughton Publishers, an Hachette UK company. All rights reserved. 'NIV' is a registered trademark of Biblica. UK trademark number 1448790.

Cover photo: Paul Go images/Lightstock

A catalogue record for this book is available from the British Library

Printed in the UK by Stephens & George Print Group

The Word was God

Short reflections for Advent

Andy John

The Prologue to John's Gospel is unlike any other part of the New Testament. In just a few verses it contains the mystery of the incarnation—how God became human. The same verses outline the fulfilment of all God's plans for his creation and provide the foundation for Christian hope.

In these short Advent reflections, one for every day between 1 December and Christmas Eve, we trace a journey through this extraordinary piece of writing. As you read and reflect on the words, let them call forth wonder and worship of the God revealed in his Son Jesus.

Gracious God, speak again, so I may hear afresh what things both great and small you wish me to hear.

IN **THE BEGINNING** was the Word, and the Word was with God, and the Word was God. He was with God in the beginning. Through him all things were made; without him nothing was made that has been made. In him was life, and that life was the light of all mankind. The light shines in the darkness, and the darkness has not understood it.

There was a man sent from God whose name was John. He came as a witness to testify concerning that light, so that through him all might believe. He himself was not the light, he came only as a witness to the light.

The true light that gives light to everyone was coming into the world. He was in the world, and though the world was made through him, the world did not recognise him. He came to that which was his own, but his own did not receive him. Yet to all who did receive him, to those who believed in his name, he gave the right to become children of

God—children born not of natural descent, nor of human decision or a husband's will, but born of God.

The Word became flesh and made his dwelling among us. We have seen his glory, the glory of the one and only Son, who came from the Father full of grace and truth.

(John testified concerning him. He cried out, saying, 'This is the one I spoke about when I said, "He who comes after me has surpassed me because he was before me."') Out of his fullness we have all received grace in place of grace already given. For the law was given through Moses; grace and truth came through Jesus Christ. No one has ever seen God, but the one and only Son, who is himself God and is in the closest relationship with the Father, has made him known.

JOHN 1:1–18

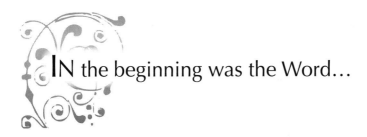 IN the beginning was the Word…

 We cannot understand what God is doing now without looking back to the beginning...

… and from the very beginning God has spoken and revealed himself.

If you can, step out into the night and look up at the stars.
The light you see has been travelling for countless years;
God's eternity stretches back further still.

… and the Word was with God, and the Word was God. He was with God in the beginning.

 The Galilean would not be another prophet
in a long line of holy people.

He would be nothing less than God, speaking God's words, doing God's works.

God stepped into human life; how might you step into the life of God?

Through him all things were made; without him nothing was made that has been made.

 God's full and unimpeded Lordship is revealed
over all creation through his Word.

Every moment, every breath, every heartbeat
is birthed in God's own being.

Lord of all, as you spoke life into existence,
speak into the smallness of our lives, so that we may
know more of your infinite greatness.

In him was life, and that life was the light of all mankind.

 The touch of the Lord Almighty ignites the spark of human life.

We are made by God, in the image of God,
to know and love God.

Step out into a busy street and look around you,
remembering that within each person burns the divine fire.

The light shines in the darkness…

 Darkness cannot extinguish light because light will always pierce the gloom...

... and so the gospel of Christ can transform hopeless lives and hopeless situations.

Bring to mind a dark place in our world and pray for God's light to scatter the shadows.

... and the darkness has not understood it.

 Darkness cannot become light or lose its obscurity by itself.

God does not abandon us, but at times we cannot sense his presence.

Come, gentle Saviour and Light of the world; shine into the places of our lives long hidden from your love.

There was a man sent from God whose name was John. He came as a witness to testify concerning that light...

 A messiah, long promised, was near and the Baptist would announce his coming.

The Word, who was with God, was speaking to his world.

How is God calling you to testify to the light today?

… so that through him all might believe.

 The purpose of John's life was pointing people to Jesus.

It is through the stories we share of God's working that faith can grow.

Think of a time when you sensed God at work in your life;
find a way to tell that story.

He himself was not the light; he came only as a witness to the light.

How often do we claim credit for something
which is not ours but God's?

John shows us that lowliness is a worthy response to Christ.

*Help us, Lord, to be content with the privilege of sharing
your gospel without seeking praise for ourselves.*

The true light that gives light to everyone was coming into the world.

 Unless we are enlightened as to who Jesus really is, we know him either partially or not at all.

The gospel is not clever teaching for the bright and sophisticated; it is redeeming grace for everyone.

If you had to summarise your faith in a sentence, what would you say?

He was in the world, and though
the world was made through him…

 The immeasurably vast became impossibly small.

The transcendent became immanent.

Reflect on the humility of God and what response it draws from you.

... the world did not recognise him.

The gospel begins with the ache in God for his creation…

… but the rejection of Jesus, witnessed in his life and death, continues still.

Heavenly Father, as your heart yearns for the world,
so grow within us hearts that beat with your compassion.

He came to that which was his own,
but his own did not receive him.

 The pain was sharpest in this most bitter of rejections…

... for, if your own people turn against you, it cuts to the heart.

Where have you experienced rejection and how have you responded?

Yet to all who did receive him,
to those who believed in his name,
he gave the right to become children
of God…

 Believing in God's name means believing all that is true about God.

Through his gracious generosity, we are welcomed into his family.

Ponder the mystery: simply believing bestows belonging.

… children born not of natural descent, nor of human decision or a husband's will, but born of God.

 A birth is always a remarkable event.

Being born into God's family is actually more remarkable still.

Loving God, deepen our wonder that, just as children are born into the world, you give birth to us.

The Word became flesh and made his dwelling among us.

 Here is the very ground of the gospel:
God has stepped into human history.

He is here for all time, in a way that he wasn't before.

Picture or describe what it means for God to be in our midst.

We have seen his glory, the glory
of the one and only Son, who came
from the Father…

 God's glory had come as cloud and fire in former times…

... but now we see that glory in the face of Jesus.

So we have seen that glory. What difference does it make?

... full of grace and truth.

 Grace and truth are not opposites.

They reside perfectly together in Jesus.

Heavenly Father, let your truth inform us and your grace transform us.

John testified concerning him. He cried out, saying, 'This is the one I spoke about when I said, "He who comes after me has surpassed me because he was before me."'

Jesus was with God before time began.

In his Lordship we find the source and purpose of life.

As the angels saw and proclaimed—and as John proclaims here—
Jesus is worthy of praise and glory, now and for ever.

Out of his fullness we have all received grace in place of grace already given.

 In God's economy there are no half measures;
there is only fullness.

His generous love contains within it immeasurable power to redeem and bless.

*Reflect on where and how God's generosity
is producing fruit in your life.*

For the law was given through Moses…

 The law required choices that reflected God's standards and showed where people fell short —and also how they could continue in faith...

… but the old revelation and ways of obedience were now transcended.

*Holy God, we thank you that, while your law exposes
our weakness, your mercy forgives our frailty.*

... grace and truth came through Jesus Christ.

 His coming puts an end to condemnation
and rejection…

… which means we are freed to live as forgiven sinners.

Let us remember each day to put down our burdens of guilt.

No one has ever seen God...

 God is hidden from our mortal eyes...

… although we are granted glimpses of his presence through creation.

*How might glimpses of God in creation lead us
to a deeper searching for him?*

… but the one and only Son, who is himself God and is in the closest relationship with the Father, has made him known.

 In the great plan of God's salvation, Jesus stands centre stage. There is no other like him, nor could there be.

So we can have true confidence in him, who is God's most precious gift to us.

Heavenly Father, in your Son Jesus you have made yourself known to us most completely. May our knowing you lead us to love and serve you in glad and grateful obedience.

Lord Jesus, thank you for the message of Christmas—for the good news that finite humanity contained the uncontainable, infinite God; that you have come to us and, from within our humanity, redeemed and saved us.

New Daylight

Sustaining your daily journey with the Bible

Andy John is a regular contributor to *New Daylight*, our most popular series of Bible reading notes. For each daily note, the full Bible text is included and the passage is explained by one of our experienced writers, helping you to understand how it is relevant to your own spiritual journey.

New Daylight is published three times a year, for January–April, May–August and September–December. It is available in print, Deluxe edition (with larger print size), app for Android, iPhone and iPad, and daily email.

For free downloadable samples of all BRF's Bible reading notes, please visit www.biblereadingnotes.org.uk/samples-and-promotional-materials.

Quiet Spaces

A creative response to God's love

Quiet Spaces is for people who enjoy exploring the Bible using their innate spirituality and creativity. Published three times a year, each issue of *Quiet Spaces* provides four months' worth of inspiration for your quiet time, presented in fortnightly sections. This material can be used in daily portions throughout the week or all in one sitting as a Quiet Day, perhaps at the weekend. Within each section there are twelve elements, comprising reflections inspired by different traditions, creative activities, liturgy, Bible reading and ideas for meditation.

Quiet Spaces is available in print.

For free downloadable samples of all BRF's Bible reading notes, please visit www.biblereadingnotes.org.uk/samples-and-promotional-materials.

The Twelve Degrees of Silence

Marie-Aimée de Jésus OCD

Edited by Lucinda M. Vardey

The stresses and strains of contemporary life leave so many of us thirsting for peace and clarity of mind and heart. This book invites us to nurture a spirituality of silence through the words and wisdom of the 19th-century Carmelite and mystic, Sister Marie-Aimée de Jésus. Through a combination of her measured insights and exercises for personal application by author and spiritual teacher Lucinda M. Vardey, the reader is invited on a twelve-movement journey into a silent and intimate union with God. An introduction and biography of Marie-Aimée de Jésus explores her influence on other well-known Carmelites such as the saint and martyr Edith Stein.

ISBN 978 0 85746 407 1   £5.99
Available from your local Christian bookshop or direct from BRF: please visit www.brfonline.org.uk

The Contemplative Minister

Learning to lead from the still centre

Ian Cowley

At one time, Christian ministry offered the opportunity to spend your life in the study of God's word, in reading and reflection, in prayer and sermon preparation, and in the faithful pastoral care of a community. These days there are very few jobs in full-time ministry which do not require a heroic combination of stamina, multi-tasking and change management. Drawing on his experience of developing and leading relevant training programmes, Ian Cowley assesses the stresses and pressures of the job and shows how to grow into a 'contemplative minister', prioritising a relationship of deepening love with God.

ISBN 978 0 85746 360 9   £8.99
Available from your local Christian bookshop or direct from BRF: please visit www.brfonline.org.uk

Also from BRF

Moments of Grace

Reflections on meeting with God

Joy MacCormick

From desolation to celebration, loneliness to love, *Moments of Grace* offers pithy, thought-provoking reflections on themes connecting God, faith and the journey of life. Questions for further pondering help the reader make links between head and heart, between what they believe, what they wrestle with believing and what they experience day by day.

ISBN 978 0 85746 224 4   £6.99
Available from your local Christian bookshop or direct from BRF: please visit www.brfonline.org.uk

Also from BRF

Journalling the Bible

40 writing exercises

Corin Child

The spiritual discipline of journalling has become increasingly popular in recent years, and this book shows how it can fruitfully overlap with creative writing, generating new insights and application even from the most familiar of Bible passages. *Journalling the Bible* offers 40 writing/journalling exercises, providing an original, imaginative way of engaging with the Bible for individuals and groups.

ISBN 978 0 84101 736 5   £7.99
Available from your local Christian bookshop or direct from BRF: please visit www.brfonline.org.uk

Enjoyed this book?

Write a review—we'd love to hear what you think. Email: reviews@brf.org.uk

Sign up for email news and select your interest groups at: www.brfonline.org.uk/findoutmore/

Follow us on Twitter @brfonline

To receive new title information by post (UK only), complete the form below and post to:
BRF Mailing Lists, 15 The Chambers, Vineyard, Abingdon, Oxfordshire, OX14 3FE

Name_____

Address_____

_____ Postcode _____

Email_____

Your interest groups (Please tick as appropriate)

- ☐ Advent/Lent
- ☐ Bible Reading & Study
- ☐ Children's Books
- ☐ Discipleship
- ☐ Leadership

- ☐ Messy Church
- ☐ Pastoral
- ☐ Prayer & Spirituality
- ☐ Resources for Children's Church
- ☐ Resources for Schools